THINGS TO DO IN SUMMER

Brighter Vision Education Ltd.
Eton House, 18-24 Paradise Road, Richmond, Surrey TW9 1SR

Copyright 1998 Brighter Vision Education Ltd.

™ is a trademark of Brighter Vision Education Ltd.

Some material used in this book is used under licence from
Frank Schaffer Publications Inc.

All rights reserved. No part of this publication may be reproduced,
stored in a retrieval system, or transmitted in any form or by any means,
electronic, mechanical, photocopying, recording or otherwise, without the prior
permission of the publisher.

This book is sold subject to the condition that it shall not, by way of trade or
otherwise, be lent, re-sold, hired out, or otherwise circulated without the
publisher's prior consent in any form of binding or cover other than that in
which it is published and without similar condition including this condition
being imposed on the subsequent purchaser.

Written by Elizabeth McKinnon and Gayle Bittinger
Illustrated by Barb Tourtillotte
Consultant Editor: Margot O'Keeffe

ACKNOWLEDGEMENTS

We would like to thank all the teachers and readers who have contributed ideas and
materials used in the preparation of this book.

Printed in Belgium

BV-05-014 Things To Do In Summer
ISBN 1 86172 124 2

INTRODUCTION

This collection of exciting ideas and activities for things to do in Summer provides a rich resource of fun-filled learning opportunities for pre-school children, both at school and at home.

The activities have been suggested with the warm days of Summer in mind, so many of them can take place outdoors. For example, there are hands-on science activities for investigating forces using outdoor climbing equipment. However, most of the ideas could be undertaken either outdoors or inside, depending on the weather at the time. Also included are language activities, songs and rhymes, together with lots of ideas for interesting and healthy snacks.

The layout of the book has been designed to be simple and accessible so that you can plan ahead and have time to prepare materials for certain activities. Use the index at the back of the book to select activities thematically, or choose activities to complement your usual curriculum and give your children interesting learning opportunities whilst having fun at the same time.

Water

HANDS-ON SCIENCE
Exploring Water
Fill plastic trays with warm water. Add toys such as those listed below and encourage your children to use them for pouring, squeezing, squirting, and sprinkling.
- plastic measuring cups
- plastic funnels
- sponges
- plastic bottles
- kitchen basters
- plastic containers with holes punched around the bottoms

MOVEMENT
Making Bubbles
Fill a bowl or a large tub with water. Let your children take turns standing by the bowl, spreading their fingers, then rapidly moving their hands back and forth in the water to make bubbles.

RHYME
Water, Water
Water, water
Everywhere,
On my face
And on my hair,
On my fingers,
On my toes.
Water, water
On my nose!

Jean Warren

SONG

Water Song

Sung to: "The Wheels on the Bus"

Oh, the water
In the cup goes
Splash, splash, splash.
Splash, splash, splash.
Splash, splash, splash.
Oh, the water
In the cup goes
Splash, splash, splash
When I pour it out.

Oh, the water
In the bottle goes
Squirt, squirt, squirt.
Squirt, squirt, squirt.
Squirt, squirt, squirt.
Oh, the water
In the bottle goes
Squirt, squirt, squirt
When I squeeze it out.

Additional verse: Oh, the water in the sponge goes drip, drip, drip when I squeeze it out.

Jean Warren

LANGUAGE IDEA

Talk with your children about different ways we use water such as for drinking, cooking, bathing, washing clothes, and watering plants.

SNACK IDEA

Let your children help mix water with juice concentrate to make a lunchtime drink.

Floating and Sinking

HANDS-ON SCIENCE

Sink or Float?
Put out a bowl filled with water. Collect several objects that float, such as a sponge, a cork and a rubber ball, and several objects that sink, such as a rock, a crayon and a metal spoon. Hold up one object at a time and ask your children to guess whether it will sink or float. Then let them place the object in the water to see if their guesses were correct.

MOVEMENT

Like a Rock
Play music and let your children pretend to be boats, rubber ducks or similar objects floating around in the water. Whenever you stop the music, let the children pretend to be rocks and sink to the floor.

RHYME

What Do You Think?
If a leaf
Falls in water,
What do you
Think?
Will the
Leaf float
Or will the
Leaf sink?

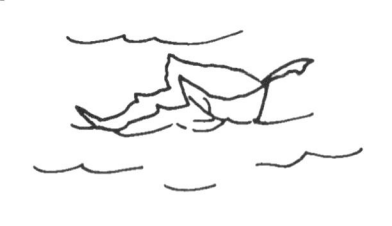

Repeat, each time substituting the name of a different object for *leaf*.

Elizabeth McKinnon

SONG

Sink and Float Song

Sung to: "Clementine"

Find a rock,
Find a rock,
Find a rock
Right now.
Put the rock
In the water.
Put it in
The water now.

Watch it sink,
Watch it sink,
Watch it sink
Right now.
Watch it sink
In the water.
Watch it sink
Right now.

Repeat, substituting the word *sponge* for *rock* and *float* for *sink*. Continue with similar verses about other objects that sink and float.

Elizabeth McKinnon

LANGUAGE IDEA

Set out objects that float and objects that sink. Make up a story about the objects as your children take turns dropping them into a tub of water.

SNACK IDEA

Serve soup with vegetables or noodles that sink and let your children float small croutons on top.

Sandals

HANDS-ON LEARNING GAME

Sandal Match
Find different kinds and sizes of sandals and place several pairs in a box. Let your children take turns sorting through the sandals to find the matching pairs. Occasionally add another pair to make the game more challenging.

MOVEMENT

Sandal Walk
Set out different kinds of sandals in large sizes. Let your children take turns trying on the sandals and walking around the room in them.

RHYME

My Sandal Shoes
My sandal shoes
Are reddish brown,
With airy holes
All around.
And when it is
A nice warm day,
I wear my sandals
Out to play.

Lois E. Putnam

SONG

Sandals

Sung to: "If You're Happy and You Know It"

Sandals keep
Our feet so cool,
Oh, so cool.
Sandals keep
Our feet so cool,
Oh, so cool.
Sandals keep
Our feet so cool
When we play
At home or school.
Sandals keep
Our feet so cool,
Oh, so cool.

Elizabeth McKinnon

LANGUAGE IDEA

Talk with your children about how sandals are like ordinary shoes and how they are different.

SNACK IDEA

Let your children wear sandals while they eat their lunch.

Buckets

HANDS-ON LEARNING GAME
Nesting Fun
Collect three or four plastic buckets that will fit one inside the other. Show your children how to nest the buckets. Then take the buckets apart and let the children take turns nesting them.

MOVEMENT
Bucket Lift
Place empty buckets on the floor. Ask your children to pretend that the buckets are full of rocks and ask them to show how they would lift the buckets. Continue by letting the children pretend that the buckets are full of other materials, such as feathers, bricks, cottonwool balls or sand.

RHYME
A Bucket
Here is a bucket
To carry about.
Fill it way up,
Then empty it out.

Elizabeth McKinnon

SONG

Bucket Song
Sung to: "Ten Little Indians"

Shovel in the sand,
Fill up your bucket.
Shovel in the sand,
Fill up your bucket.
Shovel in the sand,
Fill up your bucket.
Fill up your bucket now.

Dump out the sand,
Empty your bucket.
Dump out the sand,
Empty your bucket.
Dump out the sand,
Empty your bucket.
Empty your bucket now.

Repeat, each time substituting a different word, such as blocks or dirt, for sand.

Elizabeth McKinnon

LANGUAGE IDEA

Hide a familiar object inside a bucket. Describe the object and let your children try to guess what it is.

SNACK IDEA

Wrap snack foods in aluminium foil or cling film. Serve them to your children from a clean bucket.

11

Sand

HANDS-ON SCIENCE

Exploring Sand

Set out a bowl of sand for each of your children. Provide sand-play toys such as those listed below and let the children use them for digging, scooping, pouring and sifting.

- small shovels or spoons
- scoops
- plastic measuring cups
- plastic funnels
- plastic containers
- sifters

Extension: Let your children play in damp sand with pastry cutters.

MOVEMENT

Digging With Feet

Designate a special time in your sand area for "feet-only" digging. Let your children take off their shoes and socks. Then let them dig, design and build with their bare feet.

RHYME

Sand Everywhere

Sand on the beach.
Sand on the doll.
Sand on the bucket.
Sand on the ball.

Sand on the blanket.
Sand on the bear.
Sand on the shovel.
Sand everywhere!

Jean Warren

SONG

I Love Sand

Sung to: "Three Blind Mice"

Sand, sand, sand.
Sand, sand, sand.
I love sand.
I love sand.
It's fun to squish it
Between my toes,
Or build a mountain
As high as my nose,
Or dig a tunnel
That grows and grows,
'Cause I love sand!

Susan Hodges

LANGUAGE IDEA

Bury small toys or other familiar objects in sand. Let your children dig them up and name them.

SNACK IDEA

Make a cake for the children in the shape of a sandcastle. Put flags on it.

Scooping

HANDS-ON LEARNING GAME

Sand Scoops

Use clean plastic bleach bottles or detergent bottles to make Sand Scoops for your children. To make each one, squeeze glue around the opening of the bottle and tightly screw on the lid. Then use a craft knife to cut off the bottom of the bottle at an angle. Smooth over any rough edges. Let the children play with their scoops in sand, experimenting to see how many scoops it takes to fill various containers.

MOVEMENT

Scooping Moves

Let your children pretend to scoop up different materials using various sizes of make-believe scoops. For example, ask them to use tiny scoops to scoop up imaginary beads or giant scoops to scoop up pretend feather pillows.

RHYME

Here Is My Scoop

Here is my scoop.
Watch me go.
I scoop up the sand
Just like so.
   (Make scooping motions.)

Repeat, each time substituting a different word, such as *peas* or *dirt*, for *sand*.

Elizabeth McKinnon

SONG

Scoop and Count
Sung to: "Row, Row, Row Your Boat"

Scoop, scoop,
Scoop the sand.
Scoop it,
One, two, three.
Scooping, scooping,
Scooping, scooping,
Scoop and count
With me.

Repeat, each time substituting a different word, such as *beans* or *dirt*, for *sand*.

Elizabeth McKinnon

LANGUAGE IDEA

Place small objects on the floor and set out scoops. Give your children directions such as these: "Scoop up something red. Scoop up a toy. Scoop up something that bounces."

SNACK IDEA

Pour dry cereal into a large bowl. Let your children scoop out the cereal into smaller bowls to eat for a snack.

Shells

HANDS-ON LEARNING GAME

Shell Play

Collect various kinds and sizes of sea shells. Bury the shells in the sand and let your children dig through the sand to find them. When all the shells have been found, ask the children to line them up from smallest to largest or from largest to smallest.

MOVEMENT

Open Shells, Closed Shells

Let your children pretend to be clams living in the sea. When you call out, "Open your shells!" the children stretch their arms out at their sides. When you call out, "Close your shells!" the children raise their arms high overhead, fingers touching. Continue calling out directions as long as interest lasts.

RHYME

Sea Shells

See the pretty
Sea shells.
Count them
One by one.
Line them up
Upon the sand.
It really is
Quite fun!

Adapted Traditional

SONG

Pretty Sea Shell

Sung to: "Frère Jacques"

Pretty sea shell,
Pretty sea shell
On the sand,
On the sand.
Pick it up
And hold it,
Pick it up
And hold it
In your hand,
In your hand.

Elizabeth McKinnon

LANGUAGE IDEA

Sit with your children and pass around a sea shell. Encourage them to describe what the shell looks and feels like.

SNACK IDEA

Cook pasta shells and use them to make a soup or salad.

17

Fish

HANDS-ON ART

Fish Mural

Cut fish shapes out of white paper. Let your children decorate the shapes with crayons or felt-tip pens. Help them to glue their fish shapes onto a large piece of paper. Add twisted green crêpe-paper streamers for seaweed. Then hang the mural on a wall and cover it with blue cellophane to make an underwater scene.

MOVEMENT

Swimming Fishes

Let your children imagine that they are little fishes. Play music and let them "swim" around the room, swishing their pretend tails as they go.

RHYME

Fishies

Fishies, fishies,
Swimming round,
Sometimes up,
Sometimes down,
Sometimes fast,
Sometimes slow.
Near the net
We'd better not go!

Kathy McCullough

SONG

Fish, Fish

Sung to: "Skip to My Lou"

Fish, fish,
Swim up high.
Fish, fish,
Swim down low.
Fish, fish,
Swim so fast,
Fish, fish,
Swim so slow.

Let your children act out the movements as you sing the song.

Betty Silkunas

LANGUAGE IDEA

Glue small pictures onto fish shapes and place them in a box. As your children "fish" for the shapes, incorporate the pictures into a story you make up.

SNACK IDEA

Make some fish-shaped placemats to use at lunch time.

Crabs

HANDS-ON LEARNING GAME
Learning About Five
Hold up a picture of a crab. Help your children count five legs on one side of the crab and five legs on the other side. Then make sets of five with the children, using objects such as blocks, crayons or toy cars.

MOVEMENT
Crab Walk
Let your children pretend to be little crabs on a sandy beach. Encourage them to crawl around sideways, first going one way, then the other. (Explain that sideways is the way that crabs move.)

RHYME
A Crab
Along the beach
By the sea,
Search
As you go by.
  (Cup hand above eye.)
If you look
Quite carefully,
A crab
You'll surely spy.
  (Move hands like crab claws.)

Susan Peters

SONG

Saw a Crab

Sung to: "Clementine"

I went walking,
I went walking,
Saw a crab
Right on the beach.
Saw a crab,
Saw a crab
Walking this way
With its feet.
    (Walk sideways.)

Cindy Dingwall

LANGUAGE IDEA

Put out a cutout of a crab and several different rocks. Let your children take turns following directions such as these: "Put the crab on top of the biggest rock. Put the crab under the black rock. Put the crab beside the round rock."

SNACK IDEA

Encourage your children to use their thumbs and fingers like crab pincers when they eat their snacks.

Jobs

HANDS-ON DRAMATIC PLAY
Job Fun
Set out hats and other props used by various kinds of workers such as firefighters, police officers, builders, chefs, clowns, and football players. Let your children try on the hats and use the props as they pretend to do different jobs.

MOVEMENT
Worker Moves
Let your children pretend to be workers as you take the part of their boss. Lead them in doing various kinds of jobs, such as fighting a fire, directing traffic, building a house or making bread.

RHYME
Our Country's Workers
We work in the factories
And in the offices too.
We are the workers
All around you.

We work at the post office
And we work at the zoo.
Drivers, teachers, builders –
We work hard for you.

Brian Biddinger
Nancy Nason Biddinger

SONG

What Will You Be?
Sung to: "The Wheels on the Bus"

What will you be
When you grow up,
You grow up,
You grow up?
What will you be
When you grow up,
When you're older?

Jacob's going to be
A firefighter,
Firefighter,
Firefighter.
Jacob's going to be
A firefighter
When he's older.

Sing the song for each of your children, substituting the child's name for *Jacob* and what he or she wants to be for *firefighter*.

Frank Dally

LANGUAGE IDEA

Name several things that a particular worker does, such as bake bread, make biscuits, and ice cakes. Then ask your children to guess the worker's job (a baker).

SNACK IDEA

Give each of your children a job to do to prepare for lunch time. Include setting the table, making the snack and cleaning up afterward.

23

Boats

HANDS-ON LEARNING GAME

Colour Boat Match

Cut identical boat shapes and sail shapes out of three different colours of felt. Place the boat shapes on a flannelboard. Give the sail shapes to your children and let them take turns placing the sails above the matching-coloured boats.

MOVEMENT

Over the Waves We Go

Let your children pretend to be sitting in a large rowing boat. Sit at the front of the pretend boat and show the children how to "row" all together as the waves rock you back and forth. Then lead the children in paddling a big canoe.

RHYME

Little Boat

Look in the
Toy box.
Find a
Little boat.
Put it
In the water
And watch
It float.

Elizabeth McKinnon

SONG

Rowing

Sung to: "Row, Row, Row Your Boat"

Waves, waves,
Back and forth,
Rock the boat
All day.
    (Move hands like waves.)
We row and row
So we can go
Somewhere
Far away.
    (Pretend to row boat.)

Jean Warren

LANGUAGE IDEA

Display pictures of different kinds of boats and ask your children to tell how they are alike and how they are different.

SNACK IDEA

Wrap snack foods in aluminum foil or cling film and serve them from a large toy boat.

Trains

HANDS-ON ART
Cardboard-Box Train
Set out several cardboard boxes to use for train carriges. Let your children decorate them by drawing on designs with crayons or felt-tip pens or by gluing on crêpe-paper streamers. Line up the boxes, fasten them together with thick string, and attach a string handle to the front box. Then let the children take turns pulling stuffed-animal "passengers" around the room in their decorated train.

MOVEMENT
Chugging Trains
Use pieces of masking tape to make railway tracks on the floor. Let your children pretend to be trains and chug back and forth along the tracks while making choo-choo sounds.

RHYME
Clickety-Clack
Clickety-clack,
Clickety-clack.
See the train
On the track.

Clickety-clack,
Clickety-clack.
See the train
Going back.

Adapted Traditional

SONG

I'm a Little Red Train
Sung to: "Three Blind Mice"

I'm a little red train
Chugging down the track,
A little red train
Going up and back.
I travel all day
Going round and round,
Taking goods
From town to town.
I'm a little red train
Going down the track.
Chug, chug, chug.

Jean Warren

LANGUAGE IDEA

Tell a train story to your children. Whenever they hear the word *train*, they have to say, "Choo-choo."

SNACK IDEA

Let your children pretend to be a train and chug in a line to the lunch table.

Aeroplanes

HANDS-ON LEARNING GAME

Planes in Hangars

On a large piece of white paper, draw a red box, a yellow box, and a blue box to represent aeroplane hangars. Cut two aeroplane shapes each out of red, yellow, and blue paper. Mix up the shapes and let your children take turns placing the aeroplanes in the matching-coloured hangars.

MOVEMENT

Zooming Aeroplanes

Let your children pretend to be aeroplanes. They should hold their arms straight out at their sides and "fly" around the room while making zooming sounds. If desired, make a masking-tape runway on the floor for "take-offs" and "landings."

RHYME

In an Aeroplane

When I grow up
I'll say goodbye,
Then dart away
Into the sky.
I'll fly around
In my aeroplane,
But soon I will
Come down again.

Adapted Traditional

LANGUAGE IDEA

Display a picture of an aeroplane and name its different parts with your children.

SNACK IDEA

Let your children sit in chairs lined up to resemble an aeroplane cabin. Serve snack foods on disposable food trays.

SONG

I'm an Aeroplane
Sung to: "Clementine"

I'm an aeroplane,
I'm an aeroplane
Flying up
Into the sky.
Flying higher,
Flying higher
As I watch
The clouds go by.

I'm an aeroplane,
I'm an aeroplane.
See me flying
All around.
Flying lower,
Flying lower
Till I land
Down on the ground.

Let your children act out the movements as you sing the song.

Elizabeth McKinnon

Doing the Washing

HANDS-ON DRAMATIC PLAY

Washing Clothes

Pour warm water into bowls and add small amounts of liquid detergent. (Check first whether any of your children have sensitive skin.) Set out a basket of "laundry" that includes items such as doll clothes, face cloths, or infant shirts and socks. Let your children take turns washing the laundry. When they have finished, hang them on a clothes line.

MOVEMENT

Washing Machines

Ask your children to imagine that they are washing machines. Walk among them, pretending to put in clothes and soap. When you "turn on" the machines, they should twist and shake until the imaginary clothes inside are all clean.

RHYME

Rub, Rub, Rub

Washing clothes,
Toss 'em in the tub.
Add some soap,
Then rub, rub, rub!

Elizabeth McKinnon

SONG

This Is the Way

Sung to: "The Mulberry Bush"

This is the way
We wash the clothes,
Wash the clothes,
Wash the clothes.
This is the way
We wash the clothes,
So early
In the morning.

Repeat, each time substituting a different word, such as *socks* or *shirts* for *clothes*.

Traditional

LANGUAGE IDEA

Talk with your children about the steps in doing the washing, including sorting clothes, putting them into the washer, adding soap, and turning on the machine.

SNACK IDEA

Let your children help to wash cloth placemats. Then dry the placemats and use them on the lunch table.

Clothes line Fun

HANDS-ON LEARNING GAME

Hanging Up the Washing

Tie a clothes line between two short chairs. In a laundry basket, place items such as dolls' clothes, face cloths, or children's socks and shirts. Using clothes pegs, help your children to hang up the items by kind (first all the socks, then all the shirts, etc.). Then help them to hang up items by colour or by number.

MOVEMENT

Bell Clothesline

Using pieces of string, hang small bells at various heights from an ordinary clothes line. Let your children take turns jumping and stretching to ring the bells.

RHYME

On the Line

Wet clothes,
Wet clothes,
Hanging
On the line.
Let them
Dry
In the
Bright sunshine.

Repeat, each time substituting a different word, such as *socks* or *sheets*, for *clothes*.

Elizabeth McKinnon

SONG

On the Clothes line

Sung to: "My Bonnie Lies Over the Ocean"

Hang up the shirts
On the clothes line.
Oh, hang up the shirts
To dry.
Hang up the shirts
On the clothes line.
Oh, hang up the shirts
So high.
Hang up, hang up,
Oh, hang up the shirts
To dry, to dry.
Hang up, hang up,
Oh, hang up the shirts
So high.

Repeat, each time substituting a different word, such as *trousers* or *towels*, for *shirts*.

Gayle Bittinger

LANGUAGE IDEA

Use clothes pegs to hang various items from a low clothes line. As you describe the different items, let your children remove them from the line.

SNACK IDEA

Place snack foods in resealable plastic sandwich bags. Clip the bags to a low clothes line to serve.

Picnic Fun

HANDS-ON DRAMATIC PLAY

Picnic Play

In a picnic basket, place items such as a tablecloth, napkins, plates, cups, and spoons. Also add a few empty food containers such as yoghurt pots or plastic bottles. Let your children unpack the basket, have a pretend picnic, and then pack up the basket again.

MOVEMENT

Around the Basket

Stand with your children in a large circle. Place a picnic basket on the floor in the middle. Then move around the circle with the children as you sing the song "The Picnic Basket" (page 35).

RHYME

Picnic Basket

Picnic basket,
Open it wide.
What are some things
You see inside?

Crisps and pickles,
Sandwiches, too.
A picnic lunch
For me and you.

Elizabeth McKinnon

SONGS

Picnic in the Park
Sung to: "She'll Be Coming Round the Mountain"

Yes, we'll all go on
A picnic in the park.
Yes, we'll all go on
A picnic in the park.
Bring some lunch
And bring a ball.
There will be
Such fun for all!
Yes, we'll all go on
A picnic in the park.

Barbara Paxson

The Picnic Basket
Sung to: "The Mulberry Bush"

Here we go round
The picnic basket,
The picnic basket,
The picnic basket.
Here we go round
The picnic basket,
So early
In the morning.

Repeat, each time substituting a different action word, such as *skip*, *hop*, or *crawl*, for *go*.

Adapted Traditional

LANGUAGE IDEA

Tell your children a story about a picnic. As you do so, take items out of a picnic basket and use them as story props.

SNACK IDEA

Pack snack foods in a picnic basket and have an outdoor or an indoor picnic.

Paper Plates

HANDS-ON ART
Paper-Plate Lunches
Cut pictures of nutritious foods out of magazines. Give each of your children a paper plate. Let the children brush glue on their plates. Then let them choose food pictures and place them on top of the glue. Display the plates on paper "placemats," if desired.

MOVEMENT
Paper-Plate Toss
Collect several paper plates. Let your children stand in an open area. Give the plates to the children and let them see how far they can toss them.

RHYME
My Paper Plate
Have you seen
My paper plate,
Filled with
Things to eat?

Yes, I've seen
Your paper plate.
It's filled with
Biscuit treats.

Repeat, each time substituting a different food name for *biscuit*.

Elizabeth McKinnon

SONG

Paper Plates
Sung to: "Jingle Bells"

Paper plates,
Paper plates,
Fill them up
With treats.
Apples, oranges,
Sandwiches,
Oh, so good
To eat.
Paper plates,
Paper plates,
Add some
Biscuits, too.
See the plates
All filled up now,
Just for
Me and you.

Elizabeth McKinnon

LANGUAGE IDEA

Draw faces on paper plates and attach craft sticks for handles. Use the paper-plate puppets for telling stories.

SNACK IDEA

Serve each of your children a snack on a paper plate.

Ants

HANDS-ON SCIENCE

Observing Ants

Take your children on a walk to look for and observe ants. Or "invite" ants to come to you by placing a juicy piece of fruit outdoors on the ground. With the children, visit the site of the fruit after an hour or so to observe and talk about the ants that have discovered it. Remind your children to watch where they step so that they don't hurt the ants.

MOVEMENT

Scampering Ants

Let your children get down on their hands and knees, pretending to be little ants. Play music and let them crawl and scamper around on the floor. Whenever you stop the music, let the "ants" crawl under a table to hide in their "nest."

RHYME

Crawly Ant

See the little
Crawly ant
Walk across
The floor.
See the little
Crawly ant
Walk right to
The door.

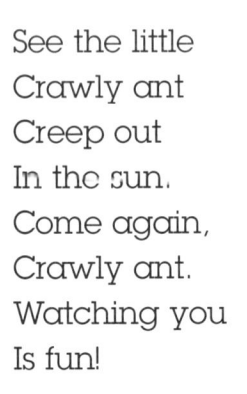

See the little
Crawly ant
Creep out
In the sun.
Come again,
Crawly ant.
Watching you
Is fun!

Beverly Qualheim

SONG

The Ants Are Busy

Sung to: "She'll Be Coming Round the Mountain"

Oh, the ants are busy,
Busy as can be.
Oh, the ants are busy,
Busy as can be.
See them scamper
Here and there,
See them scamper
Everywhere.
Oh, the ants are busy,
Busy as can be.

Oh, the ants are busy,
Busy as can be.
Oh, the ants are busy,
Busy as can be.
See them dig
And dig and dig
Lots of tunnels,
Oh, so big.
Oh, the ants are busy,
Busy as can be.

Kristine Wagoner

LANGUAGE IDEA

Make up a story about a hungry ant at a picnic. As you tell the story, let your children name foods that the ant wants to eat.

SNACK IDEA

Make "ants on logs" by filling short celery pieces with cream cheese and placing dark raisins on top.

Stars

HANDS-ON ART

Night Sky Stars

Give each child a piece of white paper. Use a white crayon to draw several stars on each paper. (Be sure to press down hard with the crayon when colouring in the stars.) Let your children brush thinned black tempera paint over their papers and watch as the stars appear in the "night sky."

MOVEMENT

Reach for the Stars

Cut star shapes out of yellow or white card and hang them from the ceiling at different heights. Let your children take turns jumping up to touch the stars.

RHYME

Wish on a Star

Star light,
Star bright,
First star
I see tonight.
I wish I may,
I wish I might
Have the wish
I wish tonight.

Traditional

SONGS

Little Stars
Sung to: "Frère Jacques"

Little stars,
Little stars,
Way up high
In the sky.
I can see
Them sparkle.
I can see
Them twinkle.
Way up high
In the sky.

Elizabeth McKinnon

The Stars Are Shining Bright
Sung to: "The Farmer in the Dell"

The stars are
Shining bright.
See their
Twinkling light.
When you see
The sky at night,
The stars are
Shining bright.

Gayle Bittinger

LANGUAGE IDEA

Cover a cardboard star shape with foil. Pass the star around and let each of your children make a wish on it.

SNACK IDEA

Serve slices of star fruit or toast made with star-shaped pastry cutters.

Twinkle, Twinkle, Little Star

HANDS-ON ART
Twinkling Stars
Make paint pads by placing folded paper towels in shallow containers and pouring on small amounts of tempera paint. Let your children press star-shaped pastry cutters on the paint pads, then on pieces of paper to make star prints. While the paint is still wet, help the children to sprinkle on glitter.

MOVEMENT
Twinkle Dancing
Let your children pretend to be stars. Attach star stickers to their fingertips. Then play music and let the children "twinkle" and dance around the room.

RHYME
Twinkle, Twinkle, Little Star
Twinkle, twinkle,
Little star.
How I wonder
What you are.
Up above the world
So high,
Like a diamond
In the sky!

Traditional

SONG

A Tiny Little Star
Sung to: "Three Blind Mice"

There's a little star
Way up in the sky.
A tiny little star
Up so very high.
It twinkles brightly
Through the night.
But during the day
It is out of sight.
There's a little star
Way up in the sky.
Tiny little star.

Jean Warren

LANGUAGE IDEA

Make a "little star" puppet. Use it for telling stories about what the star can see from "up above the world so high."

SNACK IDEA

For the lunch table, decorate paper cups and paper placemats with star stickers.

43

Tents

HANDS-ON DRAMATIC PLAY
Tent Fun
Set up a real tent for your children. Or make a tent by draping a blanket or a sheet over a clothes line. Place a sleeping bag, a torch and some plastic dishes inside the tent and let your children take turns "camping out."

MOVEMENT
In and Out the Tent
Make a tent that is open at the front and back by draping a sheet or a blanket over a table. Let your children crawl in the front of the tent and out the back as you sing the song "In and Out the Tent" (page 45).

RHYME
Here Is My Tent
Here is my tent,
Cozy as can be.
Won't you come in
And play with me?

Elizabeth McKinnon

SONGS

Crawl Inside The Tent
Sung to: "Row, Row, Row Your Boat"

Let's crawl
Inside the tent.
Let's crawl
Inside today.
When we crawl
Inside the tent,
We can laugh
And play.

Elizabeth McKinnon

In and Out the Tent
Sung to: "Go In and Out the Window"

Go in and out the tent,
Go in and out the tent.
Go in and out the tent,
As we have done before.

Let your children go in and out a real or a pretend tent while singing the song.

Adapted Traditional

LANGUAGE IDEA

Sit inside a tent with your children and read them a story.

SNACK IDEA

Let your children enjoy eating their snacks inside a tent.

Books

MOVEMENT

Act It Out

Choose a storybook that has a lot of action. Read the book to your children and let them act out the story.

HANDS-ON LEARNING GAME

Our Counting Book

Make a blank book by fastening five pieces of white paper together with a coloured paper cover. Write "Our Counting Book" on the front. Use a felt-tip pen to number the pages from 1 to 5. With your children, attach matching numbers of stickers to each page. Then give the book to the children to "read" to one another.

RHYME

My Book

Here is
My book.
I'll open
It wide
To show you
The pictures
That are
Inside.

Adapted Traditional

SONG

Take a Look

Sung to: "If You're Happy and You Know It"

Take a look,
Take a look
At my book.
Take a look,
Take a look
At my book.
Turn the pages
Nice and slow.
Look at pictures
As you go.
Take a look,
Take a look
At my book.

Elizabeth McKinnon

LANGUAGE IDEA

Sit with your children in the book corner. Talk with them about how to handle and take care of books.

SNACK IDEA

Read a favourite storybook to your children while they eat their lunch.

Cows

HANDS-ON LEARNING GAME
Cow Match
Cut six identical cow shapes out of white card. Divide them into three pairs. Use felt-tip pens to decorate each pair of cows differently. Then mix up the shapes and let your children take turns finding the matching cows.

MOVEMENT
Leading the Cows Home
With your children, pretend to be cows. Get down on all fours with the children behind you. Then lead them around the room, with them copying your movements, until you finally reach your big barn "home."

RHYME
Milk the Cow
Milk the cow,
Milk the cow
While sitting on a stool.
Pulling, squirting,
Pulling, squirting,
Till the bucket's full.

Pat Beck

SONG

What Do Cows Say?
Sung to: "London Bridge"

What do cows say?
Moo, moo, moo.
Moo, moo, moo.
Moo, moo, moo.
What do cows say?
Moo, moo, moo,
On the farm.

Cows eat grass and
Chew, chew, chew.
Chew, chew, chew.
Chew, chew, chew.
Cows eat grass and
Chew, chew, chew,
On the farm.

Additional verses: Cows give milk, that's true, true, true; I like milk, don't you, you, you?

Becky Valenick

LANGUAGE IDEA

Talk with your children about how cows give milk and how that milk is made into various dairy products.

SNACK IDEA

Serve dairy products such as milk, cheese, butter, yoghurt, or ice cream.

Wheels

HANDS-ON LEARNING GAME
Counting Wheels
Collect various kinds of toys that have wheels such as cars, lorries, wheelbarrows and tricycles. Invite your children to sit with you. Encourage them to touch and examine the wheels on the toys. Then together count the number of wheels on each toy.

MOVEMENT
Parade on Wheels
Help your children decorate riding toys with crêpe-paper streamers. Then let them ride the toys in a parade around the room or outdoors.

RHYME
Watch the Wheels
Watch the wheels
Go round and round
As we drive
Our car to town.

Repeat, each time substituting a different word, such as *lorry*, *van*, *bus* or *car*.

Judy Hall

SONG

Wheel Song

Sung to: "Old MacDonald Had a Farm"

Little Laura
Had a car.
E-I-E-I-O.
And on her car
She had some wheels.
E-I-E-I-O.
With a wheel,
Wheel here.
And a wheel,
Wheel there.
Here a wheel,
There a wheel,
Everywhere
A wheel, wheel.
Little Laura
Had a car.
E-I-E-I-O.

Sing the song for each of your children, substituting the child's name for *Laura* and the name of a different vehicle for *car*.

Jean Warren

LANGUAGE IDEA

Tell a story about wheels to your children. Let them roll their hands whenever they hear the word *wheels*.

SNACK IDEA

Place snack foods on a trolley and wheel them to the table to serve.

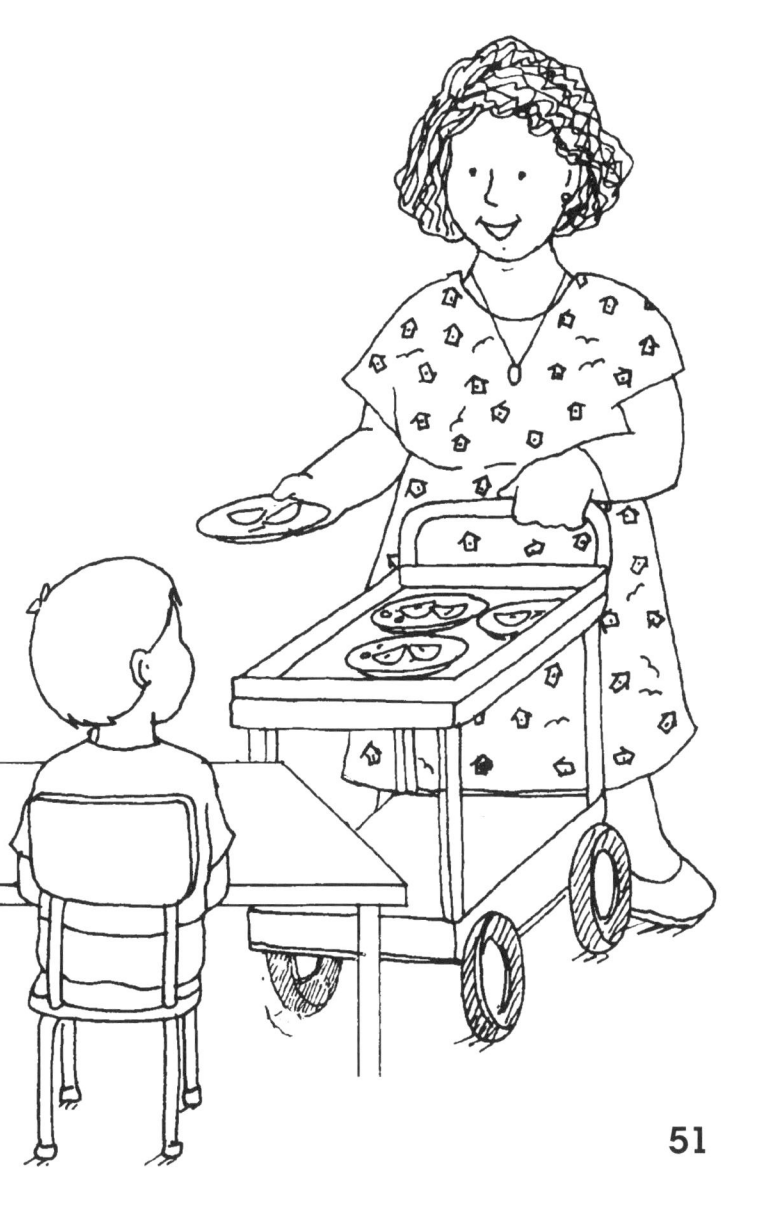

Cars

HANDS-ON LEARNING GAME
Colour Parking
Collect several different colours of toy cars. Find a large shallow box to use for a car park. In the bottom of the box, draw or glue paper rectangles in colours that match the cars. Cut a square opening in one side of the box for a door. Let your children take turns driving the cars into the car park and "parking" them on the matching-coloured rectangles.

MOVEMENT
Toy Car Fun
Use strips of masking tape to make a race track on the floor. Give your children toy cars. Let them push the cars back and forth along the track, making putt-putt sounds as they go.

RHYME
My Little Red Car
Hop aboard
My little red car.
   (Pretend to drive.)
Let's drive
Up and down.
Round and round
And round we go,
All around
The town.

Jean Warren

SONG

Riding in the Car
Sung to: "The Farmer in the Dell"

We're riding in the car.
We're riding in the car.
Heigh-ho, away we go.
We're riding in the car.

We're riding, oh, so far.
We're riding, oh, so far.
Heigh-ho, away we go.
We're riding, oh, so far.

Jean Warren

LANGUAGE IDEA

Sit with your children in a pretend car. Talk with them about what you see as you "drive" around.

SNACK IDEA

Set up a "restaurant" and let your children drive pretend cars to it for their lunch.

Lorries

MOVEMENT
Lorry Drivers
Let your children imagine that they are lorry drivers. Let them climb into their pretend lorries and "drive" around the room. Periodically, hold up a red or a green circle to signal stop or go.

HANDS-ON DRAMATIC PLAY
Loading and Unloading
Collect several toy lorries. Use masking tape to create a large road map on the floor. Make sure that the roads are wide enough for the toy lorries to travel on. Set out materials such as wooden bricks, small rocks or toy logs. Let your children load the lorries with the materials and "drive" them to different locations on the road map for unloading.

RHYME
In My Lorry
I am riding
In my lorry.
Watch me
Going past.
I am riding
In my lorry,
Going slow,
Then fast.

Gayle Bittinger

SONG

Lorry Song

Sung to: "My Bonnie Lies Over the Ocean"

I love to ride
Down the highway.
Now I will
Tell you why.
I love to look
Out the window
And watch
The lorries go by.
Lorries, lorries,
Lorries, lorries.
I watch the lorries
Go by, go by.
Lorries, lorries,
Lorries, lorries.
I watch the lorries
Go by.

Jean Warren

LANGUAGE IDEA

Display pictures of cars and lorries. Talk with your children about how the vehicles are alike and how they are different.

SNACK IDEA

Wrap snack foods in aluminum foil or cling film. Place them in a large toy lorry for delivering at lunch time.

Pet Care

HANDS-ON SCIENCE

Pet Day

Plan a Pet Day with your children. Invite them to bring in their pets – or photos of their pets – for others to see. Give each child a chance to talk about his or her pet and to tell how he or she helps care for it.

MOVEMENT

Pets and Owners

Let half your children pretend to be pet owners and let the other half pretend to be their pets. The owners do pretend activities such as feeding, walking, petting and playing with their "pets." Then let the children reverse roles.

RHYME

Our Pet

Our pet has
A special place.
We keep it clean
And neat
We feed our pet
Every day.
It really likes
To eat!

Cindy Dingwall

SONG

Love Your Pets

Sung to: "Row, Row, Row Your Boat"

Love, love,
Love your pets,
Love them
Every day.
Give them food
And water, too.
Then let them
Run and play.

Elizabeth McKinnon

LANGUAGE IDEA

Using stuffed animals as props, talk with your children about the proper way to hold, stroke and play with pets.

SNACK IDEA

Use pastry cutters to cut toast into bone shapes for "doggy snacks" and fish shapes for "pussy snacks."

Animal Homes

HANDS-ON LEARNING GAME

Matching Game

On four pairs of index cards, draw or glue pictures of familiar animals and their homes. For example, on one pair of cards, draw a dog on one card and a kennel on the other card. On another pair, draw a fish and a fishbowl. Mix up the cards. Then let your children take turns matching the pictures of the animals with the pictures of their homes.

MOVEMENT

Animals in Homes

Let your children act out different animals living in their homes, such as bears in caves, rabbits in holes, cows in barns, squirrels in trees or birds in nests.

RHYME

Houses

Here is a nest
For Mrs. Bluebird.
> (Cup hands together.)

Here is a hive
For Mr. Bee.
> (Place fists together.)

Here is a hole
For Mr. Rabbit.
> (Form circle with thumb and finger.)

And here is a house
For me.
> (Form roof shape with fingers.)

Adapted Traditional

58

SONG

Animal Homes
Sung to: "The Farmer in the Dell"

A squirrel
Lives in a tree.
A snail
Lives in a shell.
A bear lives
Inside a cave.
It suits her
Very well.

Repeat, each time substituting the name of a different animal and its home, such as *bird* and *nest* or *horse* and *barn*, for *bear* and *cave*.

Elizabeth McKinnon

LANGUAGE IDEA

Make puppets by gluing pictures of animals onto the ends of craft sticks. Use the puppets for telling stories about animals and their homes.

SNACK IDEA

Let your children pretend to be different animals and eat their lunch in their imaginary animal homes.

59

Worms

HANDS-ON ART

Worm Collages

Cook whole-wheat spaghetti noodles as directed on the package. When they have cooled, use the brown noodles for "worms." Give each of your children a paper plate. Let the children arrange the noodles on their plates any way they wish to make Worm Collages. (The starch in the noodles will help the noodles stick to the plates when dry.)

MOVEMENT

Wiggle and Squirm

Let your children lie down on the floor in an open area. As you play music, they should wiggle and squirm like little worms.

RHYME

Wiggle Worm

One day when
I was playing,
I met a
Tiny worm.
Instead of
Going straight,
He squirmed and squirmed
And squirmed.

Here, now,
Let me show you
How he
Got around.
He wiggled,
Wiggled, wiggled
All across
The ground.

Jean Warren

LANGUAGE IDEA

Make a "worm puppet" by cutting a hole in the bottom of a paper cup and sticking a finger up through it. Use the puppet to tell your children a worm story.

SNACK IDEA

Let your children decorate placemats with "worm tracks" by dipping string into paint and dragging it across pieces of paper.

SONG

Little Worm

Sung to: "Twinkle, Twinkle, Little Star"

Slowly, slowly
Turn around.
Look behind you
On the ground.
You will see
A little worm.
Careful, now,
He'll make you squirm!
Slowly, slowly
Turn around.
There's a worm
Right on the ground.

Mildred Claus

The Sun

[HANDS-ON ART]

Sun Art
Give each of your children a yellow paper circle for a sun. Set out 2cm squares of yellow crêpe paper or tissue paper. Let your children brush glue on their circles and place the paper squares on top of the glue. When the glue has dried, cut slits into the circles to make sun rays. Display the suns on a wall or a notice board, if desired.

[MOVEMENT]

Ring Around the Sun
Join hands with your children and walk in a circle as you sing the song below.

Sung to: "The Farmer in the Dell"

Oh, ring around the sun.
Oh, ring around the moon.
Oh, ring around
The great big world
As we sing this tune.

Jean Warren

[RHYME]

Bright Sun
Bright sun shining down,
    (Spread fingers and lower hands.)
Shining on the ground.
What a lovely face you have,
    (Form circle with arms.)
Yellow, big, and round!

Susan A. Miller

SONG

Sun Is Shining
Sung to: "Clementine"

Sun is shining,
Sun is shining,
Sun is shining
On the grass.
Sun is shining,
Sun is shining,
Sun is shining
On the grass.

Repeat, each time substituting a different word for *grass*.

Diane Thom

LANGUAGE IDEA

Talk with your children about fun things they can do in the sun.

SNACK IDEA

Let your children sit outdoors in the sunshine and eat their lunch.

Yellow

HANDS-ON LEARNING GAME

Yellow Match

Cut a large sun shape out of yellow card or paper. Place the shape on a table or on the floor. Set out small yellow objects for your children to discover. When they do so, let them place the objects on top of the yellow sun shape.

MOVEMENT

Yellow Means Slow

Take your children outdoors and let them run around the playground. Every now and then, hold up a circle cut from yellow paper. Whenever the children see the yellow circle, they have to slow down.

RHYME

On My Pillow

I found
A little ribbon
Lying on
My pillow.
It was a
Pretty ribbon
And it was
Coloured yellow.

Repeat, each time substituting a different word for *ribbon*.

Jean Warren

SONG

Stand Up for Yellow
Sung to: "London Bridge"

Kevin has a
Yellow shirt,
Yellow shirt,
Yellow shirt.
Kevin has a
Yellow shirt.
Stand up, Kevin.

Repeat for each of your children, substituting the name of the child for *Kevin* and the name of something yellow that the child is wearing or holding for *shirt*.

Elizabeth McKinnon

LANGUAGE IDEA

Look through a picture book with your children and ask them to name things they see that are yellow.

SNACK IDEA

Let your children help make a lemon drink for lunch time.

Vegetables

HANDS-ON LEARNING GAME

Veggie Match

On four pairs of index cards, draw or glue matching pictures of different vegetables, such as tomatoes, sweet corn, peas and carrots. Mix up the cards and place them in a pile. Let your children take turns sorting through the cards to find the matching pairs.

MOVEMENT

Vegetable Soup

Form an imaginary soup pot by standing in a circle with your children. Give each child a picture of a vegetable. Pretend to stir the soup with a giant spoon. As you do so, name a vegetable and let the children who have a picture of that vegetable jump into the pretend soup pot and dance around as they "cook." Repeat until all the vegetables are in the soup pot.

RHYME

One Potato, Two Potato

One potato,
Two potato,
Three potato,
Four.
Five potato,
Six potato,
Seven potato
More.
Eight potato,
Nine potato,
Here is ten.
Now let's start
All over
Again.

Repeat, each time substituting a different vegetable name, such as *tomato* for *potato*.

Adapted Traditional

SONG

Out in the Garden

Sung to: "Down at the Station"

Out in the garden
Early in the morning,
See the red tomatoes
All in a row.
See the happy farmer
Coming out to pick them.
Pick, pick, pick, pick.
Off he goes.

Out in the garden
Early in the morning,
See the orange carrots
All in a row.
See the happy farmer
Coming out to pick them.
Pick, pick, pick, pick.
Off she goes.

Additional verses: See the yellow peppers; See the green string beans; See the purple beetroots.

Jean Warren

LANGUAGE IDEA

Set out a basket of fresh vegetables. As your children take turns removing the vegetables, name each one with the group.

SNACK IDEA

Serve fresh vegetables with a dip made by mixing plain yoghurt with salad dressing to taste.

Fruits

HANDS-ON COOKING
Making Fruit Salad
Let your children help prepare a fruit salad. Set out fruits such as bananas, oranges, apples, strawberries and peaches. Let the children wash the fruit and help with the peeling. Let them use table knives to cut the fruit into bite-size pieces. Then let them help mix the pieces together in a large bowl.

MOVEMENT
Jammin'
Let your children dance around the room as you name different fruits. Occasionally, add the word *jam* to a fruit name. When you do so, let the children stamp their feet as if mashing the fruit into jam.

RHYME
Fruit Colours
There are many
Coloured fruits.
They're so good
For you.
Apples are red;
Let's eat a few.
Bananas are yellow;
Let's try them, too.

Repeat, substituting other fruit names and colours for those in the rhyme.

Gayle Bittinger

SONG

Fruit Treats

Sung to: "Frère Jacques"

I'm a grape,
I'm a grape,
Growing on a vine,
Growing on a vine.
If you want
Some grape juice,
If you want
Some grape juice,
Squash me fine,
Squash me fine.

I'm a strawberry,
I'm a strawberry,
Growing on the ground,
Growing on the ground.
If you want
Some jam,
If you want
Some jam,
Mash me around,
Mash me around.

I'm an orange,
I'm an orange,
Growing on a tree,
Growing on a tree.
If you want
Some orange juice,
If you want
Some orange juice,
Just squeeze me,
Just squeeze me.

Polly Reedy

LANGUAGE IDEA

Decorate different fruits to make puppets and use them for telling stories to your children.

SNACK IDEA

Let your children enjoy their home-made fruit salad from the activity Making Fruit Salad (page 68). Serve in clear-plastic cups with a vanilla yoghurt dressing.

Beanbags

HANDS-ON LEARNING GAME
Beanbags for Playing
Make beanbags in various sizes and shapes, using fabric in a variety of colours, patterns and textures. Fill the beanbags with large dried beans and stitch them securely closed. Let your children explore the beanbags. Talk with them about the different colours. Encourage the children to touch the beanbags and notice the different textures.

MOVEMENT
Beanbag Toss
Make a "target" by using felt-tip pens to draw a large clown face on a piece of paper. Cut out the face and tape it to the floor. Let your children stand near the clown face and try to toss beanbags onto it.

Variation: Let your children try to toss beanbags into a laundry basket or a similar container.

RHYME
A Beanbag
Here is
A beanbag.
I'll toss
It to you.
Please catch it
And toss it
Right back
To me, too.

Adapted Traditional

SONG

Found a Beanbag

Sung to: "Clementine"

Found a beanbag,
Found a beanbag,
Found a beanbag
Just now.
Just now I
Found a beanbag,
Found a beanbag
Just now.

Picked it up,
Picked it up,
Picked it up
Just now.
Just now I
Picked it up,
Picked it up
Just now.

Tossed that beanbag,
Tossed that beanbag,
Tossed that beanbag
Just now.
Just now I
Tossed that beanbag,
Tossed that beanbag
Just now.

Adapted Traditional

LANGUAGE IDEA

Hand out beanbags to your children. Then give directions such as these: "Put your beanbag on the floor. Put your beanbag under a chair. Put your beanbag in this box."

SNACK IDEA

Let your children try to balance beanbags on their heads as they walk to the lunch table.

Jack and Jill

HANDS-ON LEARNING GAME

A Bucket of Water

Fill a large bowl with water and add several plastic measuring cups. Give your children a small bucket. Let them fill the measuring cups with water and then pour the water into the bucket. Count with them the number of cups it takes to fill the bucket. Help them empty the bucket and then start the game again.

MOVEMENT

Jack and Jill Fun

Recite the rhyme "Jack and Jill" (this page). As you do so, let your children walk around the room, pretending to be Jack and Jill climbing a hill. When you get to the line that begins "Jack fell down," the children drop to the floor and roll and tumble about.

RHYME

Jack and Jill

Jack and Jill
Went up the hill
To fetch a pail
Of water.
Jack fell down
And broke his crown,
And Jill came
Tumbling after.

Traditional

SONG

Jack and Jill Song

Sung to: "Mary Had a Little Lamb"

Jack and Jill
Went up the hill,
Up the hill,
Up the hill.
    (Pretend to climb.)
Jack and Jill
Went up the hill
As high as
They could go.

Jack and Jill
Fell down the hill,
Down the hill,
Down the hill.
    (Tumble to floor.)
Jack and Jill
Fell down the hill,
Fell down,
Oh, so low.

Elizabeth McKinnon

LANGUAGE IDEA

Find a book of nursery rhymes. Read "Jack and Jill," along with other favourite rhymes, to your children.

SNACK IDEA

At lunch time, let your children help ladle water from a clean bucket into small cups for drinking.

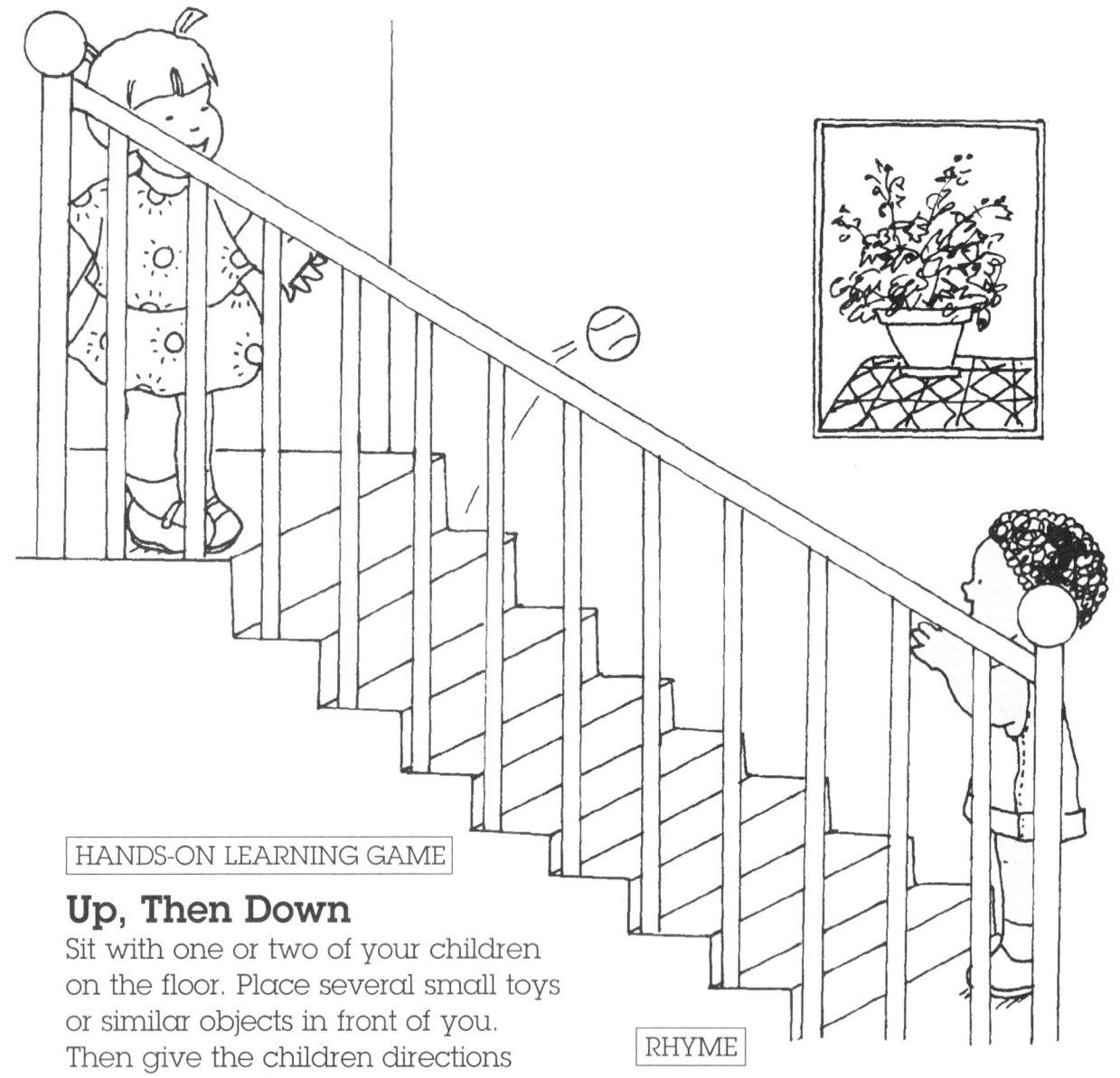

Up and Down

HANDS-ON LEARNING GAME

Up, Then Down

Sit with one or two of your children on the floor. Place several small toys or similar objects in front of you. Then give the children directions such as these: "Hold up the car. Put the car down. Hold up the brick. Put the brick down." Continue as long as interest lasts.

MOVEMENT

Up and Down

Take your children up and down stairs or a hill. Or let them toss balls or rolled-up socks up into the air and watch them come down.

RHYME

High and Low

Here's my little hand.
   (Hold out hand.)
Watch me make it go
First up so high,
   (Reach hand up.)
Then down so low.
   (Reach hand down.)

Repeat, each time substituting a different word, such as *brick, toy* or *crayon,* for *hand.*

Elizabeth McKinnon

SONGS

Put Your Hands Up
Sung to: "Mary Had a Little Lamb"

Put your hands up to the sky,
To the sky, to the sky.
Put your hands up to the sky
And see if you can fly.

Put your hands down on the floor,
On the floor, on the floor.
Put your hands down on the floor
And try to count to four.

Linda Ferguson

See Us Reach Up
Sung to: "Here We Go Looby Loo"

See us reach
Up, up, up.
See us reach
Down, down, down.
See us reach
Up, up, up.
Now see us
Twirl all around.

Elizabeth McKinnon

LANGUAGE IDEA

Put a felt hill shape on a flannelboard. Let your children take turns placing other felt shapes up on top of the hill and down at the bottom.

SNACK IDEA

At lunch time, ask your children to hold their hands up to request an item and put their hands down when they are served.

Swings

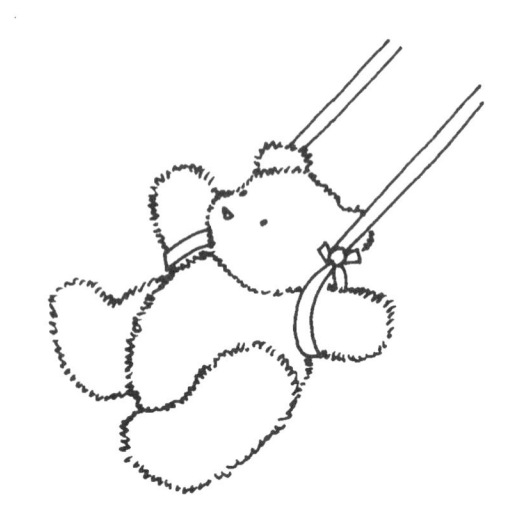

HANDS-ON DRAMATIC PLAY

Toy Swing

Select a stuffed animal, such as a bear or a rabbit. Attach wool or ribbon to its arms or around its middle. Tie the wool to a tree branch or a clothesline. Then let your children take turns pushing the stuffed toy back and forth.

MOVEMENT

Swing Fun

Take your children to a playground or a park that has swings. Let them take turns sitting in a swing as you gently push it back and forth.

RHYME

Swinging

Up and down,
Up and down
In the swing
Go I.
Up and down,
Up and down,
Swinging low,
Then high.

Jean Warren

SONG

I Am Swinging
Sung to: "Frère Jacques"

I am swinging,
I am swinging
Up so high,
Up so high.
First I swing
Forward,
Then I swing
Backward.
Touch the sky,
Touch the sky.

Susan Nydick

LANGUAGE IDEA

With your children, talk about swinging on a swing, including how it is done and how it feels.

SNACK IDEA

Let your children swing their arms up and down as they walk to the lunch table.

Slides

HANDS-ON SCIENCE
Exploring Sliding
Stand with your children around a small slide. One at a time, place different items, such as a stuffed animal, a ball, or a sponge, at the top of the slide. Ask your children to guess whether the item will go down the slide slowly or quickly. Then let go of the item and observe what happens.

MOVEMENT
Sliding Fun
Take your children to a playground or a park where there is a small slide. Let them take turns sliding down the slide while you sing the song "Sliding" (page 79).

RHYME
The Slide
Climb up the ladder.
    (Climb fingers up arm.)
Hang on to the side.
    (Grasp arm with fingers.)
Sit down at the top.
    (Place fist at top of arm.)
Then down you slide.
    (Slide fist down arm.)

Adapted Traditional

SONG

Sliding

Sung to: "Row, Row, Row Your Boat"

Climb, climb
Up the slide.
Climb up to
The top.
Sliding, sliding
Down the slide.
Slide until
You stop.

Elizabeth McKinnon

LANGUAGE IDEA

Talk with your children about slide safety tips such as these: Use only the ladder to get to the top of the slide. Slide down one at a time. Always slide down feet first.

SNACK IDEA

Let your children take turns sliding down a slide on their way to have their lunch.

INDEX

Art activities
18, 26, 36, 40, 42, 60, 62

Dramatic Play
22, 30, 34, 44, 54, 76

Language Ideas
5, 7, 9, 11, 13, 15, 17, 19, 21, 23, 25, 27, 29, 31, 33, 35, 37, 39, 41, 43, 45, 47, 49, 51, 53, 55, 57, 59, 61, 63, 65, 67, 69, 71, 73, 75, 77, 79

Learning Activities
8. 10. 16, 20, 24, 28, 32, 46, 48, 50, 52, 58, 64, 66, 68, 70, 72, 74

Movement Activities
4, 6, 8, 10, 12, 14, 16, 18, 20, 22, 24, 26, 28, 30, 32, 34, 36, 38, 40, 42, 44, 46, 48, 50, 52, 54, 56, 58, 60, 62, 64, 66, 68, 70, 72, 74, 76, 78

Rhymes
4, 6, 8, 10, 12, 14, 16, 18, 20, 22, 24, 26, 28, 30, 32, 34, 36, 38, 40, 42, 44, 46, 48, 50, 52, 54, 56, 58, 60, 62, 64, 66, 68, 70, 72, 74, 76, 78

Science Activities
4, 6, 12, 14, 38, 56, 78

Snack Ideas
5, 7, 9, 11, 13, 15, 17, 19, 21, 23, 25, 27, 29, 31, 33, 35, 37, 39, 41, 43, 45, 47, 49, 51, 53, 55, 57, 59, 61, 63, 65, 67, 69, 71, 73, 75, 77, 79

Songs
5, 7, 9, 11, 13, 15, 17, 19, 21, 23, 25, 27, 29, 31, 33, 35, 37, 39, 41, 43, 45, 47, 49, 51, 53, 55, 57, 59, 61, 63, 65, 67, 69, 71, 73, 75, 77, 79